I0765841

CRAZY FOR SUSHI

A TASTING GUIDE AND SCORE SHEETS FOR SUSHI

ELECTRIC BLUE BEE BOP PUBLISHING

Types of Sushi

Sashimi: Not actually sushi, just fish or shellfish served alone with no rice. Best type to begin a meal with.

Nigiri: A topping served on top of sushi rice, and is not a roll. Often raw or cooked fish is used, but the topping can be anything.

Maki: Rice and filling wrapped in seaweed or other wrapper. This is the sushi most people are familiar with.

Uramaki: Similar to Maki, but rice is on the outside and a wrap is around the filling. Sometimes called a backwards roll. Often drizzled with sauces or Japanese mayonnaise.

Temaki: Sushi that has been hand-rolled into a cone shape, usually eaten only by one person.

Tempura Rolls: Deep Fried Uramaki or Maki rolls, often topped with sauces. Popular with people new to trying sushi.

Inari: Deep fried tofu pouch stuffed with sushi rice and other ingredients. Can be sweet or savory. Popular with children. The corners resemble fox ears.

Oshi: Boxed pressed Sushi. The oldest form used in sushi making, made in a wooden box form. Stems from ancient method of preserving fish with rice in wood presses.

Chirashi: Served in a bowl of sushi rice with toppings scattered on top. The simplest sushi to make, and is often made in home kitchens. Toppings can be anything, not just fish.

Sushi Condiments:

Wasabi: Spicy paste made from the root of the wasabi plant, rare outside of Japan. Western wasabi is often made with horseradish and green food coloring. Aids in digestion and has anti-bacterial properties.

Soy Sauce: Used for dipping sashimi or sushi. Often mixed with wasabi, but some consider this rude. It is a personal preference.

Pickled Ginger: Used to cleanse the palate between bites of sushi, not with the sushi. Protects against food poisoning.

Types of Wraps:

Nori: The most commonly used wrap. Made of dried seaweed. Crunchy with a fishy taste.

Soy Wrap: Made of soy, usually white but can be colored with vegetables. Has a neutral taste.

Rice Paper: Made mainly of rice, occasionally wheat is added. Has a chewy texture.

Salmon Skin: Fried salmon skin. Crunchy, fatty and decadent.

Cucumber: Thinly sliced cucumber, often used in vegetarian rolls.

Perilla Leaves (Shiso): Large crisp leaves with a spicy, licorice like taste.

Abura-age Wrap: Bean Curd pouch used for Inari Sushi. The corners resemble fox ears.

Other: There are many different and creative wraps sushi chefs are using as they create new rolls, usually in fusion cuisine.

Sushi Etiquette

Some basic rules for eating sushi.

- You are usually given a warm towel at the beginning of the meal; this is for cleansing and refreshing the hands only.
- Chopsticks or fingers? Sushi was originally a finger food, so it is ok to use your hands. Sashimi is meant to be eaten with chopsticks though, since it is fish only and no rice.
- Don't fill up the saucer with soy sauce. Soy sauce is meant to compliment the fish, not over power it. If you must use soy sauce, dip the fish side in, not the rice side because it will fall apart.
- Don't add wasabi to the soy sauce either. Instead add a bit to the sushi. Often the chef has already added an amount of wasabi that they feel compliments the fish, adding too much insults the chef, plus wasabi is all you will taste.
- Pickled ginger is a palate cleanser and is meant to be eaten between bites, not placed on the sushi.
- (Note) Both wasabi and ginger have anti-bacterial properties and protect against food poisoning and indigestion.

Common Sushi Ingredients:

Ahi- Raw Tuna
Aji- Raw Spanish Mackerel
Amaebi-Sweet Shrimp (raw)
Anago-Saltwater Eel
Aoyagi-Round Clam (raw)
Bincho-Albacore White Tuna (raw)
Black Tobiko- Dyed Flying Fish Eggs
Katsuo-Skipjack Tuna (raw)
Ebi-Tiger Shrimp (cooked)
Escolar-Butterfish (raw)
Hamachi-Yellow Tail (raw)
Hamachi Toro-Yellowtail Belly (raw)
Hirame-Halibut (raw)
Hokigai-Surf Clam (cooked)
Hotate-Scallop (raw)
Ika-Squid
Ikura-Salmon Roe (fish eggs)
Iwashi-Sardine (raw)
Kani-Crab Meat (cooked)
Kanikama-Imitation Crab
Kanpachi-Amberjack (raw)
Maguro-Tuna (raw)
Masago Capelin Fish Eggs
Mirugai-Giant Clam
Saba-Mackerel (raw)
Sake-Salmon (raw)
Sake Toro-Salmon Belly (raw)
Shira Maguro-White Tuna

Tai-Red Snapper (raw)
Tako-Octopus (cooked)
Tamago-Sweet Egg Omelet (cooked)
Tobiko-Flying Fish Eggs
Toro-Blue Fin Belly (raw)
Tsubugai-Whelk Clam (raw)
Umi Masu-Ocean Trout (raw)
Unagi-Barbequed Freshwater Eel
Uni-Sea Urchin (raw)
Uzura-Quail Egg

Western Influenced and Non-Traditional Ingredients:

Bacushi-Bacon
Beef-thin sliced, raw or cooked.
Cauliflower Rice-Riced cauliflower popular with the Paleo crowd.
Cheese-used as a meat substitute, adds a complexity of flavor.
Chicken-cooked, thinly sliced or as a tempura chicken nugget.
Eggplant-Cooked and thinly sliced.
Frushi-Fruit is used.
Hamburger-cooked often with cheese for cheeseburger sushi.
Steak Tartar-thin slices of marinated beef.

Scoring:

The Bad

0-Foul: Worst Sushi ever! Spit it out before getting fish poisoning and risking your bowls exploding from painful diarrhea. The chef is one of Satan's minions or some guy pulled off the street and has no idea of food safety. The restaurant is likely a cover for some other business and isn't really a sushi place. Get out while you can and never speak of it again.

1-Dangerous and Questionable: The restaurant is a little small, smells fishy, the tables are sticky, but a friend recommended the place. Unsure of the quality of the ingredients, or if the chef washed their hands. Zero presentation, just a roll slapped on a plate. No balance between the sushi rice, fillings or toppings, Or the chef has no taste buds and created a strange combo where the flavors don't meld at all. Will not order again.

2-Bland: Tastes more machine than man made, like mass produced sushi sold in the deli section of big name stores, or the drive thru kiosk, where the fish must be pre-cooked. Unsure if vinegar was added to the rice, it is that bland. Somewhat satisfies the sushi craving but isn't worth getting again.

 # The Good 

3-Good: Effort and skill went into the making of sushi, but it is very basic. Presentation is familiar, the ingredients are decent quality, but it is a roll everyone makes. The flavors are balanced, and the rice is properly made. Satisfies the sushi craving. Will probably order again.

4-Very Good: Yummy! Taste buds zing and pop like flying fish eggs. Presentation is amazing, eye candy before eating, can't wait to dig in, but feel a little bad messing up the display. Flavors are well balanced, and a second bite is imminent. Will order again.

5-Outstanding: The chef is a true artisan and probably best kept a secret before word gets out and the sushi bar gets too crowded, or the chef moves on to bigger and better opportunities. The sushi is a rare yet perfect balance of flavors and umami, the fish melts like butter in your mouth, the seasonings play well with each other, like best friends forever. Presentation can be simplistic, honed down to reveal the true essence and meaning of the ingredients, or sophisticated and complex, telling an astonishing story as layered tastes appear and dissolve into the next mind blowing flavor. Must order again.

SUSHI NAME

SCORE:

____

Restaurant: _______________________________

Location: _________________________________

SUSHI TYPE:

- ☐ Sashimi ☐ Chirashi
- ☐ Nigiri ☐ Oshi
- ☐ Maki
- ☐ Uramaki
- ☐ Temaki
- ☐ Tempura Roll
- ☐ Inari

WRAP:

- ☐ Nori ☐ Other
- ☐ Soy ☐ None
- ☐ Rice Paper
- ☐ Salmon Skin
- ☐ Cucumber
- ☐ Shisho Leaf
- ☐ Abura-Age

MAIN INGREDIENTS:

SCORING SCALE:

```
        1     2     3     4     5
0 ──────┼─────┼─────┼─────┼─────┼──────+
```

SUSHI NAME   SCORE:

____

Restaurant:_________________________

Location: __________________________

SUSHI TYPE:

- ☐ Sashimi ☐ Chirashi
- ☐ Nigiri ☐ Oshi
- ☐ Maki
- ☐ Uramaki
- ☐ Temaki
- ☐ Tempura Roll
- ☐ Inari

WRAP:

- ☐ Nori ☐ Other
- ☐ Soy ☐ None
- ☐ Rice Paper
- ☐ Salmon Skin
- ☐ Cucumber
- ☐ Shisho Leaf
- ☐ Abura-Age

MAIN INGREDIENTS:

SCORING SCALE:

0 —|—1—|—2—|—3—|—4—|—5—|—+

SUSHI NAME

SCORE:

____

Restaurant:_____________________

Location: _______________________

SUSHI TYPE:

☐ Sashimi ☐ Chirashi

☐ Nigiri ☐ Oshi

☐ Maki

☐ Uramaki

☐ Temaki

☐ Tempura Roll

☐ Inari

WRAP:

☐ Nori ☐ Other

☐ Soy ☐ None

☐ Rice Paper

☐ Salmon Skin

☐ Cucumber

☐ Shisho Leaf

☐ Abura-Age

MAIN INGREDIENTS:

SCORING SCALE:

0 —— 1 —— 2 —— 3 —— 4 —— 5 —— +

SUSHI NAME

SCORE:

____

Restaurant:___________________________

Location: ___________________________

SUSHI TYPE:

☐ Sashimi ☐ Chirashi
☐ Nigiri ☐ Oshi
☐ Maki
☐ Uramaki
☐ Temaki
☐ Tempura Roll
☐ Inari

WRAP:

☐ Nori ☐ Other
☐ Soy ☐ None
☐ Rice Paper
☐ Salmon Skin
☐ Cucumber
☐ Shisho Leaf
☐ Abura-Age

MAIN INGREDIENTS:

SCORING SCALE:

```
        1     2     3     4     5
0 ──────┼─────┼─────┼─────┼─────┼──────  +
```

SUSHI NAME

SCORE:

____

Restaurant:_______________________

Location: _______________________

SUSHI TYPE:

- [ ] Sashimi
- [ ] Chirashi
- [ ] Nigiri
- [ ] Oshi
- [ ] Maki
- [ ] Uramaki
- [ ] Temaki
- [ ] Tempura Roll
- [ ] Inari

WRAP:

- [ ] Nori
- [ ] Other
- [ ] Soy
- [ ] None
- [ ] Rice Paper
- [ ] Salmon Skin
- [ ] Cucumber
- [ ] Shisho Leaf
- [ ] Abura-Age

MAIN INGREDIENTS:

SCORING SCALE:

```
        1    2    3    4    5
0 ——————|————|————|————|————|—————— +
```

SUSHI NAME

SCORE:

____

Restaurant: _______________________

Location: _______________________

SUSHI TYPE:

- ☐ Sashimi ☐ Chirashi
- ☐ Nigiri ☐ Oshi
- ☐ Maki
- ☐ Uramaki
- ☐ Temaki
- ☐ Tempura Roll
- ☐ Inari

WRAP:

- ☐ Nori ☐ Other
- ☐ Soy ☐ None
- ☐ Rice Paper
- ☐ Salmon Skin
- ☐ Cucumber
- ☐ Shisho Leaf
- ☐ Abura-Age

MAIN INGREDIENTS:

SCORING SCALE:

```
        1       2       3       4       5
0 ———————|———————|———————|———————|———————— +
```

SUSHI NAME

SCORE:

____

Restaurant: _______________________

Location: _______________________

SUSHI TYPE:

- ☐ Sashimi
- ☐ Chirashi
- ☐ Nigiri
- ☐ Oshi
- ☐ Maki
- ☐ Uramaki
- ☐ Temaki
- ☐ Tempura Roll
- ☐ Inari

WRAP:

- ☐ Nori
- ☐ Other
- ☐ Soy
- ☐ None
- ☐ Rice Paper
- ☐ Salmon Skin
- ☐ Cucumber
- ☐ Shisho Leaf
- ☐ Abura-Age

MAIN INGREDIENTS:

SCORING SCALE:

0 —|— 1 —|— 2 —|— 3 —|— 4 —|— 5 —|— +

SUSHI NAME   SCORE:

____

Restaurant:____________________________

Location: _____________________________

SUSHI TYPE:

☐ Sashimi ☐ Chirashi
☐ Nigiri ☐ Oshi
☐ Maki
☐ Uramaki
☐ Temaki
☐ Tempura Roll
☐ Inari

WRAP:

☐ Nori   ☐ Other
☐ Soy   ☐ None
☐ Rice Paper
☐ Salmon Skin
☐ Cucumber
☐ Shisho Leaf
☐ Abura-Age

MAIN INGREDIENTS:

SCORING SCALE:

        1   2   3   4   5
0 ——————|————|————|————|————|—————— +

SUSHI NAME

SCORE:

____

Restaurant: _______________________

Location: _________________________

SUSHI TYPE:

- ☐ Sashimi ☐ Chirashi
- ☐ Nigiri ☐ Oshi
- ☐ Maki
- ☐ Uramaki
- ☐ Temaki
- ☐ Tempura Roll
- ☐ Inari

WRAP:

- ☐ Nori ☐ Other
- ☐ Soy ☐ None
- ☐ Rice Paper
- ☐ Salmon Skin
- ☐ Cucumber
- ☐ Shisho Leaf
- ☐ Abura-Age

MAIN INGREDIENTS:

SCORING SCALE:

0 —|—1—|—2—|—3—|—4—|—5—|—+

SUSHI NAME

SCORE:

____

Restaurant: _______________________

Location: _______________________

SUSHI TYPE:

- ☐ Sashimi ☐ Chirashi
- ☐ Nigiri ☐ Oshi
- ☐ Maki
- ☐ Uramaki
- ☐ Temaki
- ☐ Tempura Roll
- ☐ Inari

WRAP:

- ☐ Nori ☐ Other
- ☐ Soy ☐ None
- ☐ Rice Paper
- ☐ Salmon Skin
- ☐ Cucumber
- ☐ Shisho Leaf
- ☐ Abura-Age

MAIN INGREDIENTS:

SCORING SCALE:

0 —— 1 —— 2 —— 3 —— 4 —— 5 —— +

SUSHI NAME

SCORE:

____

Restaurant: _______________________

Location: _______________________

SUSHI TYPE:

- [ ] Sashimi [ ] Chirashi
- [ ] Nigiri [ ] Oshi
- [ ] Maki
- [ ] Uramaki
- [ ] Temaki
- [ ] Tempura Roll
- [ ] Inari

WRAP:

- [ ] Nori [ ] Other
- [ ] Soy [ ] None
- [ ] Rice Paper
- [ ] Salmon Skin
- [ ] Cucumber
- [ ] Shisho Leaf
- [ ] Abura-Age

MAIN INGREDIENTS:

SCORING SCALE:

0 —1—2—3—4—5—+

SUSHI NAME

SCORE:

____

Restaurant: _______________________

Location: _______________________

SUSHI TYPE:

- ☐ Sashimi
- ☐ Chirashi
- ☐ Nigiri
- ☐ Oshi
- ☐ Maki
- ☐ Uramaki
- ☐ Temaki
- ☐ Tempura Roll
- ☐ Inari

WRAP:

- ☐ Nori
- ☐ Other
- ☐ Soy
- ☐ None
- ☐ Rice Paper
- ☐ Salmon Skin
- ☐ Cucumber
- ☐ Shisho Leaf
- ☐ Abura-Age

MAIN INGREDIENTS:

SCORING SCALE:

0   1   2   3   4   5   +

SUSHI NAME

SCORE:

____

Restaurant: _______________________

Location: _________________________

SUSHI TYPE:

- ☐ Sashimi ☐ Chirashi
- ☐ Nigiri ☐ Oshi
- ☐ Maki
- ☐ Uramaki
- ☐ Temaki
- ☐ Tempura Roll
- ☐ Inari

WRAP:

- ☐ Nori ☐ Other
- ☐ Soy ☐ None
- ☐ Rice Paper
- ☐ Salmon Skin
- ☐ Cucumber
- ☐ Shisho Leaf
- ☐ Abura-Age

MAIN INGREDIENTS:

SCORING SCALE:

0 —|—1—|—2—|—3—|—4—|—5—|— +

SUSHI NAME

SCORE:

____

Restaurant: _______________________

Location: _________________________

SUSHI TYPE:

- ☐ Sashimi ☐ Chirashi
- ☐ Nigiri ☐ Oshi
- ☐ Maki
- ☐ Uramaki
- ☐ Temaki
- ☐ Tempura Roll
- ☐ Inari

WRAP:

- ☐ Nori ☐ Other
- ☐ Soy ☐ None
- ☐ Rice Paper
- ☐ Salmon Skin
- ☐ Cucumber
- ☐ Shisho Leaf
- ☐ Abura-Age

MAIN INGREDIENTS:

SCORING SCALE:

```
        1     2     3     4     5
0 ──────┼─────┼─────┼─────┼─────┼────── +
```

SUSHI NAME

SCORE:

____

Restaurant: ___________________________

Location: ___________________________

SUSHI TYPE:

- ☐ Sashimi
- ☐ Chirashi
- ☐ Nigiri
- ☐ Oshi
- ☐ Maki
- ☐ Uramaki
- ☐ Temaki
- ☐ Tempura Roll
- ☐ Inari

WRAP:

- ☐ Nori
- ☐ Other
- ☐ Soy
- ☐ None
- ☐ Rice Paper
- ☐ Salmon Skin
- ☐ Cucumber
- ☐ Shisho Leaf
- ☐ Abura-Age

MAIN INGREDIENTS:

SCORING SCALE:

0 —— 1 —— 2 —— 3 —— 4 —— 5 —— +

SUSHI NAME

SCORE:

____

Restaurant:_______________________

Location: ________________________

SUSHI TYPE:

- ☐ Sashimi ☐ Chirashi
- ☐ Nigiri ☐ Oshi
- ☐ Maki
- ☐ Uramaki
- ☐ Temaki
- ☐ Tempura Roll
- ☐ Inari

WRAP:

- ☐ Nori ☐ Other
- ☐ Soy ☐ None
- ☐ Rice Paper
- ☐ Salmon Skin
- ☐ Cucumber
- ☐ Shisho Leaf
- ☐ Abura-Age

MAIN INGREDIENTS:

SCORING SCALE:

```
        1     2     3     4     5
0 ——————+—————+—————+—————+—————+—————— +
```

SUSHI NAME

SCORE:

____

Restaurant:____________________

Location: ____________________

SUSHI TYPE:

- ☐ Sashimi ☐ Chirashi
- ☐ Nigiri ☐ Oshi
- ☐ Maki
- ☐ Uramaki
- ☐ Temaki
- ☐ Tempura Roll
- ☐ Inari

WRAP:

- ☐ Nori ☐ Other
- ☐ Soy ☐ None
- ☐ Rice Paper
- ☐ Salmon Skin
- ☐ Cucumber
- ☐ Shisho Leaf
- ☐ Abura-Age

MAIN INGREDIENTS:

SCORING SCALE:

0 ——1——2——3——4——5—— +

SUSHI NAME

SCORE:

____

Restaurant: _______________________________

Location: _______________________________

SUSHI TYPE:

- ☐ Sashimi ☐ Chirashi
- ☐ Nigiri ☐ Oshi
- ☐ Maki
- ☐ Uramaki
- ☐ Temaki
- ☐ Tempura Roll
- ☐ Inari

WRAP:

- ☐ Nori ☐ Other
- ☐ Soy ☐ None
- ☐ Rice Paper
- ☐ Salmon Skin
- ☐ Cucumber
- ☐ Shisho Leaf
- ☐ Abura-Age

MAIN INGREDIENTS:

SCORING SCALE:

```
0 ——1——2——3——4——5——+
```

SUSHI NAME

SCORE:

____

Restaurant:_______________________________

Location: _______________________________

SUSHI TYPE:

- ☐ Sashimi ☐ Chirashi
- ☐ Nigiri ☐ Oshi
- ☐ Maki
- ☐ Uramaki
- ☐ Temaki
- ☐ Tempura Roll
- ☐ Inari

WRAP:

- ☐ Nori ☐ Other
- ☐ Soy ☐ None
- ☐ Rice Paper
- ☐ Salmon Skin
- ☐ Cucumber
- ☐ Shisho Leaf
- ☐ Abura-Age

MAIN INGREDIENTS:

SCORING SCALE:

0 —1—2—3—4—5—+

SUSHI NAME   SCORE:

____

Restaurant: _______________________

Location: _________________________

SUSHI TYPE:

- ☐ Sashimi ☐ Chirashi
- ☐ Nigiri ☐ Oshi
- ☐ Maki
- ☐ Uramaki
- ☐ Temaki
- ☐ Tempura Roll
- ☐ Inari

WRAP:

- ☐ Nori ☐ Other
- ☐ Soy ☐ None
- ☐ Rice Paper
- ☐ Salmon Skin
- ☐ Cucumber
- ☐ Shisho Leaf
- ☐ Abura-Age

MAIN INGREDIENTS:

SCORING SCALE:

```
        1     2     3     4     5
0 ——————+—————+—————+—————+—————+—————— +
```

SUSHI NAME

SCORE:

____

Restaurant: _______________________________

Location: _______________________________

SUSHI TYPE:

- ☐ Sashimi ☐ Chirashi
- ☐ Nigiri ☐ Oshi
- ☐ Maki
- ☐ Uramaki
- ☐ Temaki
- ☐ Tempura Roll
- ☐ Inari

WRAP:

- ☐ Nori ☐ Other
- ☐ Soy ☐ None
- ☐ Rice Paper
- ☐ Salmon Skin
- ☐ Cucumber
- ☐ Shisho Leaf
- ☐ Abura-Age

MAIN INGREDIENTS:

SCORING SCALE:

0 —— 1 —— 2 —— 3 —— 4 —— 5 —— +

SUSHI NAME

SCORE:

____

Restaurant: _______________________

Location: _________________________

SUSHI TYPE:

- ☐ Sashimi ☐ Chirashi
- ☐ Nigiri ☐ Oshi
- ☐ Maki
- ☐ Uramaki
- ☐ Temaki
- ☐ Tempura Roll
- ☐ Inari

WRAP:

- ☐ Nori ☐ Other
- ☐ Soy ☐ None
- ☐ Rice Paper
- ☐ Salmon Skin
- ☐ Cucumber
- ☐ Shisho Leaf
- ☐ Abura-Age

MAIN INGREDIENTS:

SCORING SCALE:

```
        1     2     3     4     5
0 ———————+—————+—————+—————+—————+——————— +
```

SUSHI NAME   SCORE:

____

Restaurant:___________________

Location: ___________________

SUSHI TYPE:

- ☐ Sashimi ☐ Chirashi
- ☐ Nigiri ☐ Oshi
- ☐ Maki
- ☐ Uramaki
- ☐ Temaki
- ☐ Tempura Roll
- ☐ Inari

WRAP:

- ☐ Nori ☐ Other
- ☐ Soy ☐ None
- ☐ Rice Paper
- ☐ Salmon Skin
- ☐ Cucumber
- ☐ Shisho Leaf
- ☐ Abura-Age

MAIN INGREDIENTS:

SCORING SCALE:

0 —|— 1 —|— 2 —|— 3 —|— 4 —|— 5 —|— +

SUSHI NAME

SCORE:

____

Restaurant: _______________________

Location: _______________________

SUSHI TYPE:

- ☐ Sashimi ☐ Chirashi
- ☐ Nigiri ☐ Oshi
- ☐ Maki
- ☐ Uramaki
- ☐ Temaki
- ☐ Tempura Roll
- ☐ Inari

WRAP:

- ☐ Nori ☐ Other
- ☐ Soy ☐ None
- ☐ Rice Paper
- ☐ Salmon Skin
- ☐ Cucumber
- ☐ Shisho Leaf
- ☐ Abura-Age

MAIN INGREDIENTS:

SCORING SCALE:

```
        1     2     3     4     5
0 ——————+—————+—————+—————+—————+—————— +
```

SUSHI NAME

SCORE:

____

Restaurant: _______________________

Location: _______________________

SUSHI TYPE:

- ☐ Sashimi ☐ Chirashi
- ☐ Nigiri ☐ Oshi
- ☐ Maki
- ☐ Uramaki
- ☐ Temaki
- ☐ Tempura Roll
- ☐ Inari

WRAP:

- ☐ Nori ☐ Other
- ☐ Soy ☐ None
- ☐ Rice Paper
- ☐ Salmon Skin
- ☐ Cucumber
- ☐ Shisho Leaf
- ☐ Abura-Age

MAIN INGREDIENTS:

SCORING SCALE:

```
        1     2     3     4     5
0 ——————|—————|—————|—————|—————|——————+
```

SUSHI NAME

SCORE:

____

Restaurant:_______________________

Location: _________________________

SUSHI TYPE:

- ☐ Sashimi ☐ Chirashi
- ☐ Nigiri ☐ Oshi
- ☐ Maki
- ☐ Uramaki
- ☐ Temaki
- ☐ Tempura Roll
- ☐ Inari

WRAP:

- ☐ Nori ☐ Other
- ☐ Soy ☐ None
- ☐ Rice Paper
- ☐ Salmon Skin
- ☐ Cucumber
- ☐ Shisho Leaf
- ☐ Abura-Age

MAIN INGREDIENTS:

SCORING SCALE:

0 —— 1 —— 2 —— 3 —— 4 —— 5 —— +

SUSHI NAME

SCORE:

____

Restaurant: _______________________________

Location: _________________________________

SUSHI TYPE:

☐ Sashimi ☐ Chirashi
☐ Nigiri ☐ Oshi
☐ Maki
☐ Uramaki
☐ Temaki
☐ Tempura Roll
☐ Inari

WRAP:

☐ Nori ☐ Other
☐ Soy ☐ None
☐ Rice Paper
☐ Salmon Skin
☐ Cucumber
☐ Shisho Leaf
☐ Abura-Age

MAIN INGREDIENTS:

SCORING SCALE:

```
        1     2     3     4     5
0 ———————+—————+—————+—————+—————+——————— +
```

SUSHI NAME

SCORE:

____

Restaurant: _______________________________

Location: _______________________________

SUSHI TYPE:

☐ Sashimi ☐ Chirashi

☐ Nigiri ☐ Oshi

☐ Maki

☐ Uramaki

☐ Temaki

☐ Tempura Roll

☐ Inari

WRAP:

☐ Nori ☐ Other

☐ Soy ☐ None

☐ Rice Paper

☐ Salmon Skin

☐ Cucumber

☐ Shisho Leaf

☐ Abura-Age

MAIN INGREDIENTS:

SCORING SCALE:

0	1	2	3	4	5	+

SUSHI NAME

SCORE:

____

Restaurant: _______________________

Location: _________________________

SUSHI TYPE:

☐ Sashimi ☐ Chirashi
☐ Nigiri ☐ Oshi
☐ Maki
☐ Uramaki
☐ Temaki
☐ Tempura Roll
☐ Inari

WRAP:

☐ Nori ☐ Other
☐ Soy ☐ None
☐ Rice Paper
☐ Salmon Skin
☐ Cucumber
☐ Shisho Leaf
☐ Abura-Age

MAIN INGREDIENTS:

SCORING SCALE:

0 —— 1 —— 2 —— 3 —— 4 —— 5 —— +

SUSHI NAME

SCORE:

____

Restaurant:_______________________

Location: _______________________

SUSHI TYPE:

☐ Sashimi ☐ Chirashi
☐ Nigiri ☐ Oshi
☐ Maki
☐ Uramaki
☐ Temaki
☐ Tempura Roll
☐ Inari

WRAP:

☐ Nori ☐ Other
☐ Soy ☐ None
☐ Rice Paper
☐ Salmon Skin
☐ Cucumber
☐ Shisho Leaf
☐ Abura-Age

MAIN INGREDIENTS:

SCORING SCALE:

0 —— 1 —— 2 —— 3 —— 4 —— 5 —— +

SUSHI NAME

SCORE:

____

Restaurant:_______________________________

Location: _______________________________

SUSHI TYPE:

- ☐ Sashimi ☐ Chirashi
- ☐ Nigiri ☐ Oshi
- ☐ Maki
- ☐ Uramaki
- ☐ Temaki
- ☐ Tempura Roll
- ☐ Inari

WRAP:

- ☐ Nori ☐ Other
- ☐ Soy ☐ None
- ☐ Rice Paper
- ☐ Salmon Skin
- ☐ Cucumber
- ☐ Shisho Leaf
- ☐ Abura-Age

MAIN INGREDIENTS:

SCORING SCALE:

0 —— 1 —— 2 —— 3 —— 4 —— 5 —— +

SUSHI NAME

SCORE:

____

Restaurant: _______________________

Location: _________________________

SUSHI TYPE:

- ☐ Sashimi ☐ Chirashi
- ☐ Nigiri ☐ Oshi
- ☐ Maki
- ☐ Uramaki
- ☐ Temaki
- ☐ Tempura Roll
- ☐ Inari

WRAP:

- ☐ Nori ☐ Other
- ☐ Soy ☐ None
- ☐ Rice Paper
- ☐ Salmon Skin
- ☐ Cucumber
- ☐ Shisho Leaf
- ☐ Abura-Age

MAIN INGREDIENTS:

SCORING SCALE:

0 —— 1 —— 2 —— 3 —— 4 —— 5 —— +

SUSHI NAME

SCORE:

____

Restaurant:_______________________

Location: _________________________

SUSHI TYPE:

- ☐ Sashimi ☐ Chirashi
- ☐ Nigiri ☐ Oshi
- ☐ Maki
- ☐ Uramaki
- ☐ Temaki
- ☐ Tempura Roll
- ☐ Inari

WRAP:

- ☐ Nori ☐ Other
- ☐ Soy ☐ None
- ☐ Rice Paper
- ☐ Salmon Skin
- ☐ Cucumber
- ☐ Shisho Leaf
- ☐ Abura-Age

MAIN INGREDIENTS:

SCORING SCALE:

0 —|—1—|—2—|—3—|—4—|—5—|— +

SUSHI NAME

SCORE:

____

Restaurant: _______________________

Location: _________________________

SUSHI TYPE:

- ☐ Sashimi ☐ Chirashi
- ☐ Nigiri ☐ Oshi
- ☐ Maki
- ☐ Uramaki
- ☐ Temaki
- ☐ Tempura Roll
- ☐ Inari

WRAP:

- ☐ Nori ☐ Other
- ☐ Soy ☐ None
- ☐ Rice Paper
- ☐ Salmon Skin
- ☐ Cucumber
- ☐ Shisho Leaf
- ☐ Abura-Age

MAIN INGREDIENTS:

SCORING SCALE:

0 —— 1 —— 2 —— 3 —— 4 —— 5 —— +

SUSHI NAME

SCORE:

____

Restaurant:_______________________________

Location: _________________________________

SUSHI TYPE:

- ☐ Sashimi ☐ Chirashi
- ☐ Nigiri ☐ Oshi
- ☐ Maki
- ☐ Uramaki
- ☐ Temaki
- ☐ Tempura Roll
- ☐ Inari

WRAP:

- ☐ Nori ☐ Other
- ☐ Soy ☐ None
- ☐ Rice Paper
- ☐ Salmon Skin
- ☐ Cucumber
- ☐ Shisho Leaf
- ☐ Abura-Age

MAIN INGREDIENTS:

SCORING SCALE:

0 — 1 — 2 — 3 — 4 — 5 — +

SUSHI NAME

SCORE:

____

Restaurant: _______________________

Location: _______________________

SUSHI TYPE:

- ☐ Sashimi ☐ Chirashi
- ☐ Nigiri ☐ Oshi
- ☐ Maki
- ☐ Uramaki
- ☐ Temaki
- ☐ Tempura Roll
- ☐ Inari

WRAP:

- ☐ Nori ☐ Other
- ☐ Soy ☐ None
- ☐ Rice Paper
- ☐ Salmon Skin
- ☐ Cucumber
- ☐ Shisho Leaf
- ☐ Abura-Age

MAIN INGREDIENTS:

SCORING SCALE:

0 —— 1 —— 2 —— 3 —— 4 —— 5 —— +

SUSHI NAME

SCORE:

____

Restaurant:_______________________

Location: _______________________

SUSHI TYPE:

- ☐ Sashimi ☐ Chirashi
- ☐ Nigiri ☐ Oshi
- ☐ Maki
- ☐ Uramaki
- ☐ Temaki
- ☐ Tempura Roll
- ☐ Inari

WRAP:

- ☐ Nori ☐ Other
- ☐ Soy ☐ None
- ☐ Rice Paper
- ☐ Salmon Skin
- ☐ Cucumber
- ☐ Shisho Leaf
- ☐ Abura-Age

MAIN INGREDIENTS:

SCORING SCALE:

0 —— 1 —— 2 —— 3 —— 4 —— 5 —— +

SUSHI NAME

SCORE:

____

Restaurant:_______________________________

Location: _______________________________

SUSHI TYPE:

- [ ] Sashimi
- [ ] Chirashi
- [ ] Nigiri
- [ ] Oshi
- [ ] Maki
- [ ] Uramaki
- [ ] Temaki
- [ ] Tempura Roll
- [ ] Inari

WRAP:

- [ ] Nori
- [ ] Other
- [ ] Soy
- [ ] None
- [ ] Rice Paper
- [ ] Salmon Skin
- [ ] Cucumber
- [ ] Shisho Leaf
- [ ] Abura-Age

MAIN INGREDIENTS:

SCORING SCALE:

```
        1     2     3     4     5
0 ——————+—————+—————+—————+—————+—————— +
```

SUSHI NAME

SCORE:

____

Restaurant: _______________________________

Location: _________________________________

SUSHI TYPE:

- ☐ Sashimi ☐ Chirashi
- ☐ Nigiri ☐ Oshi
- ☐ Maki
- ☐ Uramaki
- ☐ Temaki
- ☐ Tempura Roll
- ☐ Inari

WRAP:

- ☐ Nori ☐ Other
- ☐ Soy ☐ None
- ☐ Rice Paper
- ☐ Salmon Skin
- ☐ Cucumber
- ☐ Shisho Leaf
- ☐ Abura-Age

MAIN INGREDIENTS:

SCORING SCALE:

0 —|— 1 —|— 2 —|— 3 —|— 4 —|— 5 —|— +

SUSHI NAME

SCORE:

____

Restaurant:_______________________________

Location: _________________________________

SUSHI TYPE:

- ☐ Sashimi ☐ Chirashi
- ☐ Nigiri ☐ Oshi
- ☐ Maki
- ☐ Uramaki
- ☐ Temaki
- ☐ Tempura Roll
- ☐ Inari

WRAP:

- ☐ Nori ☐ Other
- ☐ Soy ☐ None
- ☐ Rice Paper
- ☐ Salmon Skin
- ☐ Cucumber
- ☐ Shisho Leaf
- ☐ Abura-Age

MAIN INGREDIENTS:

SCORING SCALE:

0 —|— 1 —|— 2 —|— 3 —|— 4 —|— 5 —|— +

SUSHI NAME

SCORE:

____

Restaurant:_____________________

Location: _____________________

SUSHI TYPE:

- ☐ Sashimi ☐ Chirashi
- ☐ Nigiri ☐ Oshi
- ☐ Maki
- ☐ Uramaki
- ☐ Temaki
- ☐ Tempura Roll
- ☐ Inari

WRAP:

- ☐ Nori ☐ Other
- ☐ Soy ☐ None
- ☐ Rice Paper
- ☐ Salmon Skin
- ☐ Cucumber
- ☐ Shisho Leaf
- ☐ Abura-Age

MAIN INGREDIENTS:

SCORING SCALE:

0 —— 1 —— 2 —— 3 —— 4 —— 5 —— +

SUSHI NAME

SCORE:

____

Restaurant:_______________________

Location: _______________________

SUSHI TYPE:
☐ Sashimi ☐ Chirashi
☐ Nigiri ☐ Oshi
☐ Maki
☐ Uramaki
☐ Temaki
☐ Tempura Roll
☐ Inari

WRAP:
☐ Nori   ☐ Other
☐ Soy   ☐ None
☐ Rice Paper
☐ Salmon Skin
☐ Cucumber
☐ Shisho Leaf
☐ Abura-Age

MAIN INGREDIENTS:

SCORING SCALE:
0   1   2   3   4   5   +

SUSHI NAME

SCORE:

____

Restaurant:_______________________________

Location: _______________________________

SUSHI TYPE:

- ☐ Sashimi ☐ Chirashi
- ☐ Nigiri ☐ Oshi
- ☐ Maki
- ☐ Uramaki
- ☐ Temaki
- ☐ Tempura Roll
- ☐ Inari

WRAP:

- ☐ Nori ☐ Other
- ☐ Soy ☐ None
- ☐ Rice Paper
- ☐ Salmon Skin
- ☐ Cucumber
- ☐ Shisho Leaf
- ☐ Abura-Age

MAIN INGREDIENTS:

SCORING SCALE:

```
        1    2    3    4    5
0───────┼────┼────┼────┼────────+
```

SUSHI NAME

SCORE:

____

Restaurant: _______________________

Location: _______________________

SUSHI TYPE:

- ☐ Sashimi
- ☐ Chirashi
- ☐ Nigiri
- ☐ Oshi
- ☐ Maki
- ☐ Uramaki
- ☐ Temaki
- ☐ Tempura Roll
- ☐ Inari

WRAP:

- ☐ Nori
- ☐ Other
- ☐ Soy
- ☐ None
- ☐ Rice Paper
- ☐ Salmon Skin
- ☐ Cucumber
- ☐ Shisho Leaf
- ☐ Abura-Age

MAIN INGREDIENTS:

SCORING SCALE:

0 —|—1—|—2—|—3—|—4—|—5—|— +

SUSHI NAME

SCORE:

____

Restaurant: ___________________________________

Location: ___________________________________

SUSHI TYPE:

- ☐ Sashimi ☐ Chirashi
- ☐ Nigiri ☐ Oshi
- ☐ Maki
- ☐ Uramaki
- ☐ Temaki
- ☐ Tempura Roll
- ☐ Inari

WRAP:

- ☐ Nori ☐ Other
- ☐ Soy ☐ None
- ☐ Rice Paper
- ☐ Salmon Skin
- ☐ Cucumber
- ☐ Shisho Leaf
- ☐ Abura-Age

MAIN INGREDIENTS:

SCORING SCALE:

```
        1     2     3     4     5
0 ───────┼─────┼─────┼─────┼─────┼─────── +
```

SUSHI NAME

SCORE:

____

Restaurant:_______________________________

Location: _______________________________

SUSHI TYPE:

- [ ] Sashimi
- [ ] Chirashi
- [ ] Nigiri
- [ ] Oshi
- [ ] Maki
- [ ] Uramaki
- [ ] Temaki
- [ ] Tempura Roll
- [ ] Inari

WRAP:

- [ ] Nori
- [ ] Other
- [ ] Soy
- [ ] None
- [ ] Rice Paper
- [ ] Salmon Skin
- [ ] Cucumber
- [ ] Shisho Leaf
- [ ] Abura-Age

MAIN INGREDIENTS:

SCORING SCALE:

0 —— 1 —— 2 —— 3 —— 4 —— 5 —— +

SUSHI NAME

SCORE:

____

Restaurant:_______________________

Location: _________________________

SUSHI TYPE:

☐ Sashimi ☐ Chirashi

☐ Nigiri ☐ Oshi

☐ Maki

☐ Uramaki

☐ Temaki

☐ Tempura Roll

☐ Inari

WRAP:

☐ Nori ☐ Other

☐ Soy ☐ None

☐ Rice Paper

☐ Salmon Skin

☐ Cucumber

☐ Shisho Leaf

☐ Abura-Age

MAIN INGREDIENTS:

SCORING SCALE:

0 —— 1 —— 2 —— 3 —— 4 —— 5 —— +

SUSHI NAME

SCORE:

____

Restaurant:_______________________

Location: _________________________

SUSHI TYPE:

☐ Sashimi ☐ Chirashi

☐ Nigiri ☐ Oshi

☐ Maki

☐ Uramaki

☐ Temaki

☐ Tempura Roll

☐ Inari

WRAP:

☐ Nori ☐ Other

☐ Soy ☐ None

☐ Rice Paper

☐ Salmon Skin

☐ Cucumber

☐ Shisho Leaf

☐ Abura-Age

MAIN INGREDIENTS:

SCORING SCALE:

0 —— 1 —— 2 —— 3 —— 4 —— 5 —— +

SUSHI NAME

SCORE:

____

Restaurant: _______________________________

Location: _________________________________

SUSHI TYPE:

- ☐ Sashimi ☐ Chirashi
- ☐ Nigiri ☐ Oshi
- ☐ Maki
- ☐ Uramaki
- ☐ Temaki
- ☐ Tempura Roll
- ☐ Inari

WRAP:

- ☐ Nori ☐ Other
- ☐ Soy ☐ None
- ☐ Rice Paper
- ☐ Salmon Skin
- ☐ Cucumber
- ☐ Shisho Leaf
- ☐ Abura-Age

MAIN INGREDIENTS:

SCORING SCALE:

0 —— 1 —— 2 —— 3 —— 4 —— 5 —— +

SUSHI NAME

SCORE:

____

Restaurant:_______________________________

Location: _______________________________

SUSHI TYPE:

- ☐ Sashimi ☐ Chirashi
- ☐ Nigiri ☐ Oshi
- ☐ Maki
- ☐ Uramaki
- ☐ Temaki
- ☐ Tempura Roll
- ☐ Inari

WRAP:

- ☐ Nori ☐ Other
- ☐ Soy ☐ None
- ☐ Rice Paper
- ☐ Salmon Skin
- ☐ Cucumber
- ☐ Shisho Leaf
- ☐ Abura-Age

MAIN INGREDIENTS:

SCORING SCALE:

0 —— 1 —— 2 —— 3 —— 4 —— 5 —— +

SUSHI NAME

SCORE:

____

Restaurant: ___________________________________

Location: ___________________________________

SUSHI TYPE:

- ☐ Sashimi ☐ Chirashi
- ☐ Nigiri ☐ Oshi
- ☐ Maki
- ☐ Uramaki
- ☐ Temaki
- ☐ Tempura Roll
- ☐ Inari

WRAP:

- ☐ Nori ☐ Other
- ☐ Soy ☐ None
- ☐ Rice Paper
- ☐ Salmon Skin
- ☐ Cucumber
- ☐ Shisho Leaf
- ☐ Abura-Age

MAIN INGREDIENTS:

SCORING SCALE:

```
        1     2     3     4     5
0 ——————|—————|—————|—————|—————|—————+
```

SUSHI NAME

SCORE:

____

Restaurant:______________________________

Location: _______________________________

SUSHI TYPE:
- ☐ Sashimi ☐ Chirashi
- ☐ Nigiri ☐ Oshi
- ☐ Maki
- ☐ Uramaki
- ☐ Temaki
- ☐ Tempura Roll
- ☐ Inari

WRAP:
- ☐ Nori ☐ Other
- ☐ Soy ☐ None
- ☐ Rice Paper
- ☐ Salmon Skin
- ☐ Cucumber
- ☐ Shisho Leaf
- ☐ Abura-Age

MAIN INGREDIENTS:

SCORING SCALE:

0 —— 1 —— 2 —— 3 —— 4 —— 5 —— +

SUSHI NAME

SCORE:

____

Restaurant:_______________________

Location: _______________________

SUSHI TYPE:

- ☐ Sashimi ☐ Chirashi
- ☐ Nigiri ☐ Oshi
- ☐ Maki
- ☐ Uramaki
- ☐ Temaki
- ☐ Tempura Roll
- ☐ Inari

WRAP:

- ☐ Nori ☐ Other
- ☐ Soy ☐ None
- ☐ Rice Paper
- ☐ Salmon Skin
- ☐ Cucumber
- ☐ Shisho Leaf
- ☐ Abura-Age

MAIN INGREDIENTS:

SCORING SCALE:

0 —— 1 —— 2 —— 3 —— 4 —— 5 —— +

SUSHI NAME

SCORE:

____

Restaurant:_______________________________

Location: _________________________________

SUSHI TYPE:

- [ ] Sashimi
- [ ] Chirashi
- [ ] Nigiri
- [ ] Oshi
- [ ] Maki
- [ ] Uramaki
- [ ] Temaki
- [ ] Tempura Roll
- [ ] Inari

WRAP:

- [ ] Nori
- [ ] Other
- [ ] Soy
- [ ] None
- [ ] Rice Paper
- [ ] Salmon Skin
- [ ] Cucumber
- [ ] Shisho Leaf
- [ ] Abura-Age

MAIN INGREDIENTS:

SCORING SCALE:

0 ——1——2——3——4——5—— +

SUSHI NAME

SCORE:

____

Restaurant:_______________________

Location: _________________________

SUSHI TYPE:

- ☐ Sashimi ☐ Chirashi
- ☐ Nigiri ☐ Oshi
- ☐ Maki
- ☐ Uramaki
- ☐ Temaki
- ☐ Tempura Roll
- ☐ Inari

WRAP:

- ☐ Nori ☐ Other
- ☐ Soy ☐ None
- ☐ Rice Paper
- ☐ Salmon Skin
- ☐ Cucumber
- ☐ Shisho Leaf
- ☐ Abura-Age

MAIN INGREDIENTS:

SCORING SCALE:

```
      1     2     3     4     5
0 ────┼─────┼─────┼─────┼─────┼──── +
```

SUSHI NAME

SCORE:

____

Restaurant: _______________________

Location: _________________________

SUSHI TYPE:

- ☐ Sashimi ☐ Chirashi
- ☐ Nigiri ☐ Oshi
- ☐ Maki
- ☐ Uramaki
- ☐ Temaki
- ☐ Tempura Roll
- ☐ Inari

WRAP:

- ☐ Nori ☐ Other
- ☐ Soy ☐ None
- ☐ Rice Paper
- ☐ Salmon Skin
- ☐ Cucumber
- ☐ Shisho Leaf
- ☐ Abura-Age

MAIN INGREDIENTS:

SCORING SCALE:

0 ———|——|——|——|——|——— +
    1   2   3   4   5

SUSHI NAME

SCORE:

____

Restaurant: _______________________________

Location: _________________________________

SUSHI TYPE:

- ☐ Sashimi ☐ Chirashi
- ☐ Nigiri ☐ Oshi
- ☐ Maki
- ☐ Uramaki
- ☐ Temaki
- ☐ Tempura Roll
- ☐ Inari

WRAP:

- ☐ Nori ☐ Other
- ☐ Soy ☐ None
- ☐ Rice Paper
- ☐ Salmon Skin
- ☐ Cucumber
- ☐ Shisho Leaf
- ☐ Abura-Age

MAIN INGREDIENTS:

SCORING SCALE:

0 —— 1 —— 2 —— 3 —— 4 —— 5 —— +

<table>
<tr><td>SUSHI NAME</td><td>SCORE:</td></tr>
</table>

____

Restaurant: ___________________

Location: ___________________

SUSHI TYPE:

- ☐ Sashimi ☐ Chirashi
- ☐ Nigiri ☐ Oshi
- ☐ Maki
- ☐ Uramaki
- ☐ Temaki
- ☐ Tempura Roll
- ☐ Inari

WRAP:

- ☐ Nori ☐ Other
- ☐ Soy ☐ None
- ☐ Rice Paper
- ☐ Salmon Skin
- ☐ Cucumber
- ☐ Shisho Leaf
- ☐ Abura-Age

MAIN INGREDIENTS:

SCORING SCALE:

```
        1     2     3     4     5
0 ——————+—————+—————+—————+—————+—————— +
```

SUSHI NAME

SCORE:

____

Restaurant:______________________________

Location: ______________________________

SUSHI TYPE:

- [ ] Sashimi
- [ ] Chirashi
- [ ] Nigiri
- [ ] Oshi
- [ ] Maki
- [ ] Uramaki
- [ ] Temaki
- [ ] Tempura Roll
- [ ] Inari

WRAP:

- [ ] Nori
- [ ] Other
- [ ] Soy
- [ ] None
- [ ] Rice Paper
- [ ] Salmon Skin
- [ ] Cucumber
- [ ] Shisho Leaf
- [ ] Abura-Age

MAIN INGREDIENTS:

SCORING SCALE:

0 —— 1 —— 2 —— 3 —— 4 —— 5 —— +

SUSHI NAME

SCORE:

____

Restaurant: _______________________

Location: _________________________

SUSHI TYPE:

- ☐ Sashimi ☐ Chirashi
- ☐ Nigiri ☐ Oshi
- ☐ Maki
- ☐ Uramaki
- ☐ Temaki
- ☐ Tempura Roll
- ☐ Inari

WRAP:

- ☐ Nori ☐ Other
- ☐ Soy ☐ None
- ☐ Rice Paper
- ☐ Salmon Skin
- ☐ Cucumber
- ☐ Shisho Leaf
- ☐ Abura-Age

MAIN INGREDIENTS:

SCORING SCALE:

0 —— 1 —— 2 —— 3 —— 4 —— 5 —— +

SUSHI NAME   SCORE:

____

Restaurant: _______________________

Location: _________________________

SUSHI TYPE:
- ☐ Sashimi ☐ Chirashi
- ☐ Nigiri ☐ Oshi
- ☐ Maki
- ☐ Uramaki
- ☐ Temaki
- ☐ Tempura Roll
- ☐ Inari

WRAP:
- ☐ Nori ☐ Other
- ☐ Soy ☐ None
- ☐ Rice Paper
- ☐ Salmon Skin
- ☐ Cucumber
- ☐ Shisho Leaf
- ☐ Abura-Age

MAIN INGREDIENTS:

SCORING SCALE:

0 ——— 1 ——— 2 ——— 3 ——— 4 ——— 5 ——— +

SUSHI NAME

SCORE:

____

Restaurant:_______________________________

Location: _________________________________

SUSHI TYPE:

☐ Sashimi ☐ Chirashi

☐ Nigiri ☐ Oshi

☐ Maki

☐ Uramaki

☐ Temaki

☐ Tempura Roll

☐ Inari

WRAP:

☐ Nori ☐ Other

☐ Soy ☐ None

☐ Rice Paper

☐ Salmon Skin

☐ Cucumber

☐ Shisho Leaf

☐ Abura-Age

MAIN INGREDIENTS:

SCORING SCALE:

0 —|—1—|—2—|—3—|—4—|—5—|— +

SUSHI NAME

SCORE:

____

Restaurant: _______________________

Location: _________________________

SUSHI TYPE:

- ☐ Sashimi
- ☐ Chirashi
- ☐ Nigiri
- ☐ Oshi
- ☐ Maki
- ☐ Uramaki
- ☐ Temaki
- ☐ Tempura Roll
- ☐ Inari

WRAP:

- ☐ Nori
- ☐ Other
- ☐ Soy
- ☐ None
- ☐ Rice Paper
- ☐ Salmon Skin
- ☐ Cucumber
- ☐ Shisho Leaf
- ☐ Abura-Age

MAIN INGREDIENTS:

SCORING SCALE:

0   1   2   3   4   5   +

<table>
<tr><td>

SUSHI NAME

____

Restaurant: _______________

Location: _______________

</td><td>

SCORE:

</td></tr>
</table>

SUSHI TYPE:

☐ Sashimi ☐ Chirashi
☐ Nigiri ☐ Oshi
☐ Maki
☐ Uramaki
☐ Temaki
☐ Tempura Roll
☐ Inari

WRAP:

☐ Nori ☐ Other
☐ Soy ☐ None
☐ Rice Paper
☐ Salmon Skin
☐ Cucumber
☐ Shisho Leaf
☐ Abura-Age

MAIN INGREDIENTS:

SCORING SCALE:

```
         1     2     3     4     5
0 ───────┼─────┼─────┼─────┼─────┼─────── +
```

SUSHI NAME

SCORE:

____

Restaurant:_______________________________

Location: _______________________________

SUSHI TYPE:

- ☐ Sashimi ☐ Chirashi
- ☐ Nigiri ☐ Oshi
- ☐ Maki
- ☐ Uramaki
- ☐ Temaki
- ☐ Tempura Roll
- ☐ Inari

WRAP:

- ☐ Nori ☐ Other
- ☐ Soy ☐ None
- ☐ Rice Paper
- ☐ Salmon Skin
- ☐ Cucumber
- ☐ Shisho Leaf
- ☐ Abura-Age

MAIN INGREDIENTS:

SCORING SCALE:

```
         1     2     3     4     5
0 ———————|—————|—————|—————|—————|——————— +
```

SUSHI NAME   SCORE:

____

Restaurant:_____________________

Location: ______________________

SUSHI TYPE:

☐ Sashimi ☐ Chirashi
☐ Nigiri ☐ Oshi
☐ Maki
☐ Uramaki
☐ Temaki
☐ Tempura Roll
☐ Inari

WRAP:

☐ Nori   ☐ Other
☐ Soy   ☐ None
☐ Rice Paper
☐ Salmon Skin
☐ Cucumber
☐ Shisho Leaf
☐ Abura-Age

MAIN INGREDIENTS:

SCORING SCALE:

```
        1    2    3    4    5
0 ──────┼────┼────┼────┼────┼────── +
```

SUSHI NAME

SCORE:

____

Restaurant:____________________

Location: _____________________

SUSHI TYPE:

- ☐ Sashimi ☐ Chirashi
- ☐ Nigiri ☐ Oshi
- ☐ Maki
- ☐ Uramaki
- ☐ Temaki
- ☐ Tempura Roll
- ☐ Inari

WRAP:

- ☐ Nori ☐ Other
- ☐ Soy ☐ None
- ☐ Rice Paper
- ☐ Salmon Skin
- ☐ Cucumber
- ☐ Shisho Leaf
- ☐ Abura-Age

MAIN INGREDIENTS:

SCORING SCALE:

0 — 1 — 2 — 3 — 4 — 5 — +

SUSHI NAME

SCORE:

____

Restaurant: _______________________________

Location: _______________________________

SUSHI TYPE:

☐ Sashimi ☐ Chirashi
☐ Nigiri ☐ Oshi
☐ Maki
☐ Uramaki
☐ Temaki
☐ Tempura Roll
☐ Inari

WRAP:

☐ Nori ☐ Other
☐ Soy ☐ None
☐ Rice Paper
☐ Salmon Skin
☐ Cucumber
☐ Shisho Leaf
☐ Abura-Age

MAIN INGREDIENTS:

SCORING SCALE:

0 —— 1 —— 2 —— 3 —— 4 —— 5 —— +

SUSHI NAME

SCORE:

____

Restaurant:_______________________________

Location: _________________________________

SUSHI TYPE:

- ☐ Sashimi ☐ Chirashi
- ☐ Nigiri ☐ Oshi
- ☐ Maki
- ☐ Uramaki
- ☐ Temaki
- ☐ Tempura Roll
- ☐ Inari

WRAP:

- ☐ Nori ☐ Other
- ☐ Soy ☐ None
- ☐ Rice Paper
- ☐ Salmon Skin
- ☐ Cucumber
- ☐ Shisho Leaf
- ☐ Abura-Age

MAIN INGREDIENTS:

SCORING SCALE:

```
          1     2     3     4     5
0 ————————|—————|—————|—————|—————|———————— +
```

SUSHI NAME

SCORE:

____

Restaurant:_______________________

Location: _________________________

SUSHI TYPE:

☐ Sashimi ☐ Chirashi
☐ Nigiri ☐ Oshi
☐ Maki
☐ Uramaki
☐ Temaki
☐ Tempura Roll
☐ Inari

WRAP:

☐ Nori ☐ Other
☐ Soy ☐ None
☐ Rice Paper
☐ Salmon Skin
☐ Cucumber
☐ Shisho Leaf
☐ Abura-Age

MAIN INGREDIENTS:

SCORING SCALE:

0 —|—1—|—2—|—3—|—4—|—5—|— +

SUSHI NAME

SCORE:

____

Restaurant: _______________________

Location: _______________________

SUSHI TYPE:

- ☐ Sashimi ☐ Chirashi
- ☐ Nigiri ☐ Oshi
- ☐ Maki
- ☐ Uramaki
- ☐ Temaki
- ☐ Tempura Roll
- ☐ Inari

WRAP:

- ☐ Nori ☐ Other
- ☐ Soy ☐ None
- ☐ Rice Paper
- ☐ Salmon Skin
- ☐ Cucumber
- ☐ Shisho Leaf
- ☐ Abura-Age

MAIN INGREDIENTS:

SCORING SCALE:

```
          1     2     3     4     5
  0 ──────┼─────┼─────┼─────┼─────┼──────  +
```

SUSHI NAME

SCORE:

____

Restaurant:_______________________

Location: _______________________

SUSHI TYPE:

- ☐ Sashimi ☐ Chirashi
- ☐ Nigiri ☐ Oshi
- ☐ Maki
- ☐ Uramaki
- ☐ Temaki
- ☐ Tempura Roll
- ☐ Inari

WRAP:

- ☐ Nori ☐ Other
- ☐ Soy ☐ None
- ☐ Rice Paper
- ☐ Salmon Skin
- ☐ Cucumber
- ☐ Shisho Leaf
- ☐ Abura-Age

MAIN INGREDIENTS:

SCORING SCALE:

```
        1     2     3     4     5
0  ——————|—————|—————|—————|—————|——————  +
```

SUSHI NAME

SCORE:

____

Restaurant:_______________________________

Location: _______________________________

SUSHI TYPE:

- ☐ Sashimi ☐ Chirashi
- ☐ Nigiri ☐ Oshi
- ☐ Maki
- ☐ Uramaki
- ☐ Temaki
- ☐ Tempura Roll
- ☐ Inari

WRAP:

- ☐ Nori ☐ Other
- ☐ Soy ☐ None
- ☐ Rice Paper
- ☐ Salmon Skin
- ☐ Cucumber
- ☐ Shisho Leaf
- ☐ Abura-Age

MAIN INGREDIENTS:

SCORING SCALE:

0 —— 1 —— 2 —— 3 —— 4 —— 5 —— +

SUSHI NAME

SCORE:

____

Restaurant:____________________________

Location: ______________________________

SUSHI TYPE:

- ☐ Sashimi
- ☐ Chirashi
- ☐ Nigiri
- ☐ Oshi
- ☐ Maki
- ☐ Uramaki
- ☐ Temaki
- ☐ Tempura Roll
- ☐ Inari

WRAP:

- ☐ Nori
- ☐ Other
- ☐ Soy
- ☐ None
- ☐ Rice Paper
- ☐ Salmon Skin
- ☐ Cucumber
- ☐ Shisho Leaf
- ☐ Abura-Age

MAIN INGREDIENTS:

SCORING SCALE:

```
         1     2     3     4     5
0 ———————+—————+—————+—————+—————+——————— +
```

SUSHI NAME

SCORE:

____

Restaurant: _______________________________

Location: _________________________________

SUSHI TYPE:

- ☐ Sashimi ☐ Chirashi
- ☐ Nigiri ☐ Oshi
- ☐ Maki
- ☐ Uramaki
- ☐ Temaki
- ☐ Tempura Roll
- ☐ Inari

WRAP:

- ☐ Nori ☐ Other
- ☐ Soy ☐ None
- ☐ Rice Paper
- ☐ Salmon Skin
- ☐ Cucumber
- ☐ Shisho Leaf
- ☐ Abura-Age

MAIN INGREDIENTS:

SCORING SCALE:

0 — 1 — 2 — 3 — 4 — 5 — +

SUSHI NAME

SCORE:

____

Restaurant:_______________________

Location: _______________________

SUSHI TYPE:

- ☐ Sashimi ☐ Chirashi
- ☐ Nigiri ☐ Oshi
- ☐ Maki
- ☐ Uramaki
- ☐ Temaki
- ☐ Tempura Roll
- ☐ Inari

WRAP:

- ☐ Nori ☐ Other
- ☐ Soy ☐ None
- ☐ Rice Paper
- ☐ Salmon Skin
- ☐ Cucumber
- ☐ Shisho Leaf
- ☐ Abura-Age

MAIN INGREDIENTS:

SCORING SCALE:

0 —|— 1 —|— 2 —|— 3 —|— 4 —|— 5 —|— +

SUSHI NAME

SCORE:

____

Restaurant: _______________________

Location: _________________________

SUSHI TYPE:

- ☐ Sashimi   ☐ Chirashi
- ☐ Nigiri   ☐ Oshi
- ☐ Maki
- ☐ Uramaki
- ☐ Temaki
- ☐ Tempura Roll
- ☐ Inari

WRAP:

- ☐ Nori   ☐ Other
- ☐ Soy   ☐ None
- ☐ Rice Paper
- ☐ Salmon Skin
- ☐ Cucumber
- ☐ Shisho Leaf
- ☐ Abura-Age

MAIN INGREDIENTS:

SCORING SCALE:

```
        1    2    3    4    5
0 ——————+————+————+————+————+—————— +
```

SUSHI NAME

SCORE:

____

Restaurant: _______________________

Location: _________________________

SUSHI TYPE:

☐ Sashimi ☐ Chirashi
☐ Nigiri ☐ Oshi
☐ Maki
☐ Uramaki
☐ Temaki
☐ Tempura Roll
☐ Inari

WRAP:

☐ Nori ☐ Other
☐ Soy ☐ None
☐ Rice Paper
☐ Salmon Skin
☐ Cucumber
☐ Shisho Leaf
☐ Abura-Age

MAIN INGREDIENTS:

SCORING SCALE:

0 —|— 1 —|— 2 —|— 3 —|— 4 —|— 5 —|— +

SUSHI NAME

SCORE:

____

Restaurant:_____________________________

Location: ______________________________

SUSHI TYPE:

- ☐ Sashimi
- ☐ Chirashi
- ☐ Nigiri
- ☐ Oshi
- ☐ Maki
- ☐ Uramaki
- ☐ Temaki
- ☐ Tempura Roll
- ☐ Inari

WRAP:

- ☐ Nori
- ☐ Other
- ☐ Soy
- ☐ None
- ☐ Rice Paper
- ☐ Salmon Skin
- ☐ Cucumber
- ☐ Shisho Leaf
- ☐ Abura-Age

MAIN INGREDIENTS:

SCORING SCALE:

0 —— 1 —— 2 —— 3 —— 4 —— 5 —— +

SUSHI NAME

SCORE:

____

Restaurant:_______________________

Location: _______________________

SUSHI TYPE:

- ☐ Sashimi ☐ Chirashi
- ☐ Nigiri ☐ Oshi
- ☐ Maki
- ☐ Uramaki
- ☐ Temaki
- ☐ Tempura Roll
- ☐ Inari

WRAP:

- ☐ Nori ☐ Other
- ☐ Soy ☐ None
- ☐ Rice Paper
- ☐ Salmon Skin
- ☐ Cucumber
- ☐ Shisho Leaf
- ☐ Abura-Age

MAIN INGREDIENTS:

SCORING SCALE:

0 —— 1 —— 2 —— 3 —— 4 —— 5 —— +

SUSHI NAME

SCORE:

____

Restaurant: _______________________

Location: _________________________

SUSHI TYPE:

- ☐ Sashimi ☐ Chirashi
- ☐ Nigiri ☐ Oshi
- ☐ Maki
- ☐ Uramaki
- ☐ Temaki
- ☐ Tempura Roll
- ☐ Inari

WRAP:

- ☐ Nori ☐ Other
- ☐ Soy ☐ None
- ☐ Rice Paper
- ☐ Salmon Skin
- ☐ Cucumber
- ☐ Shisho Leaf
- ☐ Abura-Age

MAIN INGREDIENTS:

SCORING SCALE:

```
        1     2     3     4     5
0 ——————+—————+—————+—————+—————+—————— +
```

SUSHI NAME

SCORE:

____

Restaurant: _______________________________

Location: _______________________________

SUSHI TYPE:

- ☐ Sashimi ☐ Chirashi
- ☐ Nigiri ☐ Oshi
- ☐ Maki
- ☐ Uramaki
- ☐ Temaki
- ☐ Tempura Roll
- ☐ Inari

WRAP:

- ☐ Nori ☐ Other
- ☐ Soy ☐ None
- ☐ Rice Paper
- ☐ Salmon Skin
- ☐ Cucumber
- ☐ Shisho Leaf
- ☐ Abura-Age

MAIN INGREDIENTS:

SCORING SCALE:

0 —— 1 —— 2 —— 3 —— 4 —— 5 —— +

SUSHI NAME
SCORE:

____

Restaurant: _______________________

Location: _______________________

SUSHI TYPE:

- ☐ Sashimi ☐ Chirashi
- ☐ Nigiri ☐ Oshi
- ☐ Maki
- ☐ Uramaki
- ☐ Temaki
- ☐ Tempura Roll
- ☐ Inari

WRAP:

- ☐ Nori ☐ Other
- ☐ Soy ☐ None
- ☐ Rice Paper
- ☐ Salmon Skin
- ☐ Cucumber
- ☐ Shisho Leaf
- ☐ Abura-Age

MAIN INGREDIENTS:

SCORING SCALE:

0 —— 1 —— 2 —— 3 —— 4 —— 5 —— +

SUSHI NAME

SCORE:

____

Restaurant: _______________________

Location: _________________________

SUSHI TYPE:

- [ ] Sashimi
- [ ] Chirashi
- [ ] Nigiri
- [ ] Oshi
- [ ] Maki
- [ ] Uramaki
- [ ] Temaki
- [ ] Tempura Roll
- [ ] Inari

WRAP:

- [ ] Nori
- [ ] Other
- [ ] Soy
- [ ] None
- [ ] Rice Paper
- [ ] Salmon Skin
- [ ] Cucumber
- [ ] Shisho Leaf
- [ ] Abura-Age

MAIN INGREDIENTS:

SCORING SCALE:

```
        1     2     3     4     5
0 ——————+—————+—————+—————+—————+—————— +
```

SUSHI NAME

SCORE:

____

Restaurant:_______________________________

Location: _______________________________

SUSHI TYPE:

- [ ] Sashimi
- [ ] Chirashi
- [ ] Nigiri
- [ ] Oshi
- [ ] Maki
- [ ] Uramaki
- [ ] Temaki
- [ ] Tempura Roll
- [ ] Inari

WRAP:

- [ ] Nori
- [ ] Other
- [ ] Soy
- [ ] None
- [ ] Rice Paper
- [ ] Salmon Skin
- [ ] Cucumber
- [ ] Shisho Leaf
- [ ] Abura-Age

MAIN INGREDIENTS:

SCORING SCALE:

0 —— 1 —— 2 —— 3 —— 4 —— 5 —— +

SUSHI NAME   SCORE:

____

Restaurant:_____________________________

Location: _______________________________

SUSHI TYPE:
- [ ] Sashimi [ ] Chirashi
- [ ] Nigiri [ ] Oshi
- [ ] Maki
- [ ] Uramaki
- [ ] Temaki
- [ ] Tempura Roll
- [ ] Inari

WRAP:
- [ ] Nori [ ] Other
- [ ] Soy [ ] None
- [ ] Rice Paper
- [ ] Salmon Skin
- [ ] Cucumber
- [ ] Shisho Leaf
- [ ] Abura-Age

MAIN INGREDIENTS:

SCORING SCALE:

0 ——1——2——3——4——5——+

SUSHI NAME

SCORE:

____

Restaurant: ______________________

Location: ________________________

SUSHI TYPE:

- ☐ Sashimi ☐ Chirashi
- ☐ Nigiri ☐ Oshi
- ☐ Maki
- ☐ Uramaki
- ☐ Temaki
- ☐ Tempura Roll
- ☐ Inari

WRAP:

- ☐ Nori ☐ Other
- ☐ Soy ☐ None
- ☐ Rice Paper
- ☐ Salmon Skin
- ☐ Cucumber
- ☐ Shisho Leaf
- ☐ Abura-Age

MAIN INGREDIENTS:

SCORING SCALE:

0 —— 1 —— 2 —— 3 —— 4 —— 5 —— +

SUSHI NAME

SCORE:

____

Restaurant:___________________________

Location: ___________________________

SUSHI TYPE:

- ☐ Sashimi ☐ Chirashi
- ☐ Nigiri ☐ Oshi
- ☐ Maki
- ☐ Uramaki
- ☐ Temaki
- ☐ Tempura Roll
- ☐ Inari

WRAP:

- ☐ Nori ☐ Other
- ☐ Soy ☐ None
- ☐ Rice Paper
- ☐ Salmon Skin
- ☐ Cucumber
- ☐ Shisho Leaf
- ☐ Abura-Age

MAIN INGREDIENTS:

SCORING SCALE:

```
        1       2       3       4       5
0 ——————+———————+———————+———————+———————+—————— +
```

SUSHI NAME

SCORE:

____

Restaurant: _______________________________

Location: _______________________________

SUSHI TYPE:

- [ ] Sashimi
- [ ] Chirashi
- [ ] Nigiri
- [ ] Oshi
- [ ] Maki
- [ ] Uramaki
- [ ] Temaki
- [ ] Tempura Roll
- [ ] Inari

WRAP:

- [ ] Nori
- [ ] Other
- [ ] Soy
- [ ] None
- [ ] Rice Paper
- [ ] Salmon Skin
- [ ] Cucumber
- [ ] Shisho Leaf
- [ ] Abura-Age

MAIN INGREDIENTS:

SCORING SCALE:

0 —— 1 —— 2 —— 3 —— 4 —— 5 —— +

SUSHI NAME

SCORE:

____

Restaurant: _______________________

Location: _________________________

SUSHI TYPE:

- ☐ Sashimi ☐ Chirashi
- ☐ Nigiri ☐ Oshi
- ☐ Maki
- ☐ Uramaki
- ☐ Temaki
- ☐ Tempura Roll
- ☐ Inari

WRAP:

- ☐ Nori ☐ Other
- ☐ Soy ☐ None
- ☐ Rice Paper
- ☐ Salmon Skin
- ☐ Cucumber
- ☐ Shisho Leaf
- ☐ Abura-Age

MAIN INGREDIENTS:

SCORING SCALE:

0 —|—1—|—2—|—3—|—4—|—5—|— +

SUSHI NAME

SCORE:

____

Restaurant:_______________________________

Location: ________________________________

SUSHI TYPE:

- ☐ Sashimi ☐ Chirashi
- ☐ Nigiri ☐ Oshi
- ☐ Maki
- ☐ Uramaki
- ☐ Temaki
- ☐ Tempura Roll
- ☐ Inari

WRAP:

- ☐ Nori ☐ Other
- ☐ Soy ☐ None
- ☐ Rice Paper
- ☐ Salmon Skin
- ☐ Cucumber
- ☐ Shisho Leaf
- ☐ Abura-Age

MAIN INGREDIENTS:

SCORING SCALE:

0 —|—1—|—2—|—3—|—4—|—5—|— +

SUSHI NAME

SCORE:

____

Restaurant: _______________________

Location: _________________________

SUSHI TYPE:

- ☐ Sashimi ☐ Chirashi
- ☐ Nigiri ☐ Oshi
- ☐ Maki
- ☐ Uramaki
- ☐ Temaki
- ☐ Tempura Roll
- ☐ Inari

WRAP:

- ☐ Nori ☐ Other
- ☐ Soy ☐ None
- ☐ Rice Paper
- ☐ Salmon Skin
- ☐ Cucumber
- ☐ Shisho Leaf
- ☐ Abura-Age

MAIN INGREDIENTS:

SCORING SCALE:

0 —— 1 —— 2 —— 3 —— 4 —— 5 —— +

SUSHI NAME

SCORE:

____

Restaurant:_______________________________

Location: _______________________________

SUSHI TYPE:

- [ ] Sashimi
- [ ] Chirashi
- [ ] Nigiri
- [ ] Oshi
- [ ] Maki
- [ ] Uramaki
- [ ] Temaki
- [ ] Tempura Roll
- [ ] Inari

WRAP:

- [ ] Nori
- [ ] Other
- [ ] Soy
- [ ] None
- [ ] Rice Paper
- [ ] Salmon Skin
- [ ] Cucumber
- [ ] Shisho Leaf
- [ ] Abura-Age

MAIN INGREDIENTS:

SCORING SCALE:

0 —— 1 —— 2 —— 3 —— 4 —— 5 —— +

SUSHI NAME

SCORE:

____

Restaurant:_______________________

Location: _______________________

SUSHI TYPE:

- ☐ Sashimi ☐ Chirashi
- ☐ Nigiri ☐ Oshi
- ☐ Maki
- ☐ Uramaki
- ☐ Temaki
- ☐ Tempura Roll
- ☐ Inari

WRAP:

- ☐ Nori ☐ Other
- ☐ Soy ☐ None
- ☐ Rice Paper
- ☐ Salmon Skin
- ☐ Cucumber
- ☐ Shisho Leaf
- ☐ Abura-Age

MAIN INGREDIENTS:

SCORING SCALE:

0 —— 1 —— 2 —— 3 —— 4 —— 5 —— +

SUSHI NAME

SCORE:

____

Restaurant: _______________________________

Location: _______________________________

SUSHI TYPE:

- ☐ Sashimi ☐ Chirashi
- ☐ Nigiri ☐ Oshi
- ☐ Maki
- ☐ Uramaki
- ☐ Temaki
- ☐ Tempura Roll
- ☐ Inari

WRAP:

- ☐ Nori ☐ Other
- ☐ Soy ☐ None
- ☐ Rice Paper
- ☐ Salmon Skin
- ☐ Cucumber
- ☐ Shisho Leaf
- ☐ Abura-Age

MAIN INGREDIENTS:

SCORING SCALE:

0 —|—1—|—2—|—3—|—4—|—5—|— +

SUSHI NAME	SCORE:

____

Restaurant: _______________________

Location: _______________________

SUSHI TYPE:

- ☐ Sashimi ☐ Chirashi
- ☐ Nigiri ☐ Oshi
- ☐ Maki
- ☐ Uramaki
- ☐ Temaki
- ☐ Tempura Roll
- ☐ Inari

WRAP:

- ☐ Nori ☐ Other
- ☐ Soy ☐ None
- ☐ Rice Paper
- ☐ Salmon Skin
- ☐ Cucumber
- ☐ Shisho Leaf
- ☐ Abura-Age

MAIN INGREDIENTS:

SCORING SCALE:

```
          1     2     3     4     5
  0 ———————|—————|—————|—————|—————|——————— +
```

SUSHI NAME

SCORE:

____

Restaurant:_______________________

Location: _______________________

SUSHI TYPE:

- ☐ Sashimi ☐ Chirashi
- ☐ Nigiri ☐ Oshi
- ☐ Maki
- ☐ Uramaki
- ☐ Temaki
- ☐ Tempura Roll
- ☐ Inari

WRAP:

- ☐ Nori ☐ Other
- ☐ Soy ☐ None
- ☐ Rice Paper
- ☐ Salmon Skin
- ☐ Cucumber
- ☐ Shisho Leaf
- ☐ Abura-Age

MAIN INGREDIENTS:

SCORING SCALE:

0 —— 1 —— 2 —— 3 —— 4 —— 5 —— +

SUSHI NAME

SCORE:

____

Restaurant: _______________________

Location: _________________________

SUSHI TYPE:

☐ Sashimi ☐ Chirashi
☐ Nigiri ☐ Oshi
☐ Maki
☐ Uramaki
☐ Temaki
☐ Tempura Roll
☐ Inari

WRAP:

☐ Nori   ☐ Other
☐ Soy   ☐ None
☐ Rice Paper
☐ Salmon Skin
☐ Cucumber
☐ Shisho Leaf
☐ Abura-Age

MAIN INGREDIENTS:

SCORING SCALE:

0 ———1———2———3———4———5——— +

SUSHI NAME

SCORE:

____

Restaurant:______________________

Location: ________________________

SUSHI TYPE:

- ☐ Sashimi ☐ Chirashi
- ☐ Nigiri ☐ Oshi
- ☐ Maki
- ☐ Uramaki
- ☐ Temaki
- ☐ Tempura Roll
- ☐ Inari

WRAP:

- ☐ Nori ☐ Other
- ☐ Soy ☐ None
- ☐ Rice Paper
- ☐ Salmon Skin
- ☐ Cucumber
- ☐ Shisho Leaf
- ☐ Abura-Age

MAIN INGREDIENTS:

SCORING SCALE:

0 —— 1 —— 2 —— 3 —— 4 —— 5 —— +

SUSHI NAME

SCORE:

____

Restaurant: _______________________________

Location: _______________________________

SUSHI TYPE:

☐ Sashimi ☐ Chirashi
☐ Nigiri ☐ Oshi
☐ Maki
☐ Uramaki
☐ Temaki
☐ Tempura Roll
☐ Inari

WRAP:

☐ Nori ☐ Other
☐ Soy ☐ None
☐ Rice Paper
☐ Salmon Skin
☐ Cucumber
☐ Shisho Leaf
☐ Abura-Age

MAIN INGREDIENTS:

SCORING SCALE:

0 —— 1 —— 2 —— 3 —— 4 —— 5 —— +

FAVORITE SUSHIS

FAVORITE SUSHIS

FAVORITE SUSHIS

FAVORITE SUSHIS

FAVORITE SUSHIS